WHEN WOMEN WEEP

GOD RESTORES:
Discover the Power of Your Tears

By
Deborah Victoria Burrus

Copyright © 2012 by Deborah Victoria Burrus

When Women Weep
by Deborah Victoria Burrus

Printed in the United States of America

ISBN 9781624198182

All rights reserved solely by the author. The author guarantees all contents are original and do not infringe upon the legal rights of any other person or work. No part of this book may be reproduced in any form without the permission of the author. The views expressed in this book are not necessarily those of the publisher.

Unless otherwise indicated, Bible quotations are taken from the King James version of the Bible. Copyright © 1986, 1994 by the Moody Bible Institute of Chicago.

www.xulonpress.com

Kingdom Blessings

Love
Deborah V. Burn

Table of Contents

Dedication vii
Acknowledgments ix
Introduction xi

Chapter 1: Heart Matters 15
Chapter 2: Breaking the Fallow Ground 19
Chapter 3: Afflictions 23
Chapter 4: Emotions 27
Chapter 5: Love 29

Dedication

This book is dedicated in memory of my son, Dante Antoine Coleman, who inspired me to complete this work.

Acknowledgments

I am blessed to have a great support system that is filled with love, inspiration, care and compassion. I say thank you to my family, my friends and all the special ladies whose lives have been touched because of our encounters. Thank you for allowing me to be a part of your life. I love you all.

Introduction

We can hear a cry for help many times in the way in which a woman weeps. Unfortunately, for many of us, we don't always allow others to hear these cries. The pains and struggles of life silence our weeping so that we sometimes forget to feel. We learn this behavior at an early age. As children we are taught what and how to feel. I remember a time in my childhood when I wanted to share what I thought was some very important information about what a family member had done to me—only to hear my grandmother say, "You must hush and never whisper a word to anyone." From that point on I began to hush about a lot of things. Instead of talking about them I learned to weep. I wept in good times and bad. I learned that weeping kept me from suppressing those feelings I could not control.

I have often thought about Eve, the mother of all living, and how she must have felt that dreadful day Satan deceived her. How could she stand in the presence of the Creator when He called out to her? What words could she say? Would they have made a difference? After all, until then she had only felt what was good. Now she would feel both good and evil. How could she have known this act of disobedience would change the course of her life forever? "Unto the woman he said, I will greatly multiply thy sorrow and thy conception; in sorrow thou shalt bring forth children; and thy desire shall be to thy husband, and he shall rule over thee" (Genesis 3:16). Prior to this pronouncement, Adam and Eve were co-equal inhabitants of the garden. Now she would not only feel pain, but her husband would rule over her. I ask the question, what would you have done?

I don't know about you, but I think my only course of action would have been to weep. I would have wept and kept weeping. I believe Eve wept. And we as women today continue to weep. We don't discuss it, but we do. We have learned how to weep within our spirits so no one else knows. I have learned, however, that something happens when women weep.

Weeping is a specific type of human behavior that, although defined as a physiological phenomenon, has been viewed as a manifestation of emotion.

It is said to be a language that enables people to communicate their emotional status without words. In both the Old and New Testaments weeping was performed collectively during mourning rituals to communicate sadness and provide a controlled emotional release so the community could begin to heal itself after a death. People also wept for their sins, hoping their god would see and hear their tears and grant them forgiveness.

If it were possible to cure evils by lamentation and raise the dead with tears, then gold would probably be less valuable than weeping.

How many times have you shed tears over loved ones or life situations only to discover those tears were to no avail? How many times have you cried about a particular situation only to realize no more tears were left? You probably feel as if you could cry right now.

God has created us so that no matter what the circumstances are we can find a way to release all that is within us. And one way is through tears.

In my encounters with women going through trials and tribulations, I have often recommended a good cry to make them feel better. Unfortunately we struggle to hold back the tears for fear of someone knowing what we are experiencing.

My suggestion is to take a nice hot shower and while the water is running down your face allow your tears to flow. There is no end to the release you will feel as your tears are mixed with the soothing, running water.

We don't allow ourselves to weep for several reasons: 1) weeping reminds us of our pain; 2) weeping may cause us to feel weak; 3) weeping may make us feel bound to our situations.

When Mary Magdalene encountered Jesus, she washed His feet with her tears. Now that was a lot of weeping.

God created tear ducts so that we can release those things within

Introduction

us, good and bad. Weeping keeps us sane. We are not designed to hold everything inside us. We must at some time or another discover the power of releasing that which is within us by looking at matters of the heart.

My prayer is that as you read through the pages of this book you too will learn there is freedom in weeping, the likes of which you may not have realized before. It is God's desire to free us from the pains of the past, to walk with us in the present and to prepare us for the future.

It's time to discover the power of your tears.

Chapter 1

Heart Matters

"A new heart also will I give you, and a new spirit will I put within you: and I will take away the stony heart out of your flesh, and I will give you an heart of flesh." Ezekiel 36:26

When we want to get serious about something we talk about getting to the heart of the matter. For me this meant looking within to uncover some deeply rooted situations that had left my heart wounded, damaged, broken and scarred. The traumas in my life caused so much pain I felt as if I were walking around with a knife stuck in me. It seemed as if the pain would never go away. I had a huge hole in my heart that wore me down. I lost focus on who I was and began to make wrong choices. Someone once wrote a song titled "What becomes of the brokenhearted?" My heart was broken, and weeping couldn't fix it. I needed surgery.

The heart, according to the Bible, is the center not only of spiritual activity but of all life's operations. It is the home of the personal life and the seat of the conscience. It is naturally wicked and hence contaminates the whole life and character. Too often we believe the only function of the heart is to feel someone say, "I love you."

The Bible instructs us to "keep thy heart with all diligence; for out of it are the issues of life. (Proverbs 4:23)." The heart has two primary functions: physical and spiritual. The physical function of the heart is to pump blood and oxygen through our bodies so we might continue to live. When the heart becomes damaged, a skilled surgeon must repair the damage. This requires a painstaking process of using manmade instruments to cut the breastbone to get to the heart. The surgeon must then locate the damaged part(s), lift the heart from the body, tie off the blood supply to make the necessary repairs before placing the heart back into the body.

The spiritual function of the heart allows the breath of God and the blood of Jesus Christ to flow through our spirits so we might continue to live spiritually. Jesus came that we might have life and have it more abundantly. When the spiritual heart becomes damaged, due to the negative emotions of life, God (Elohim) is the only one who can make the incision and repair the damage. His incision, unlike that of mortal man, speaks healing into our hearts by His Word and His blood. His repair of the heart causes us to yearn and seek after Him. Unfortunately for many of us we are unaware of how badly our spiritual hearts are damaged, so we go through life thinking everything is okay or accepting who we are because we do not believe we can change.

When we don't think we can go on, if we would ask God to heal us the pain would begin to cease and the weeping would stop.

I was unaware of the damage to my own heart. I tried for years and years to cover the pain I felt inside. You know those pains— anger from abuse, bitterness for being rejected, hurt from lack of love. I tried to find solace in everything imaginable—drugs, illegal and legal, alcohol, sex—but nothing could do it. That's right. You have tried to nullify pain with some of these same things. Psychiatry helped, but it could not cure me. I tried anything I could think of to take away the pain. Those things only anesthetized the pain, but they couldn't take it away.

Not until I learned God was the only one who could heal my heart did I discover my weeping was not in vain. The more I wept, the closer I felt drawn to God. God became my source of inspiration.

This was not an overnight process, though. I don't want you to get the impression I just clicked my heels together three times, said, "There's no place like home," and my world fell into place. I experienced many nights of sheer horror. I was afraid to live, but I didn't want to die.

When God began to heal me, I was reminded of those events in my life that had me messed up. I had pushed them into the recesses of my mind, never to be remembered again. My heart was broken or shattered into many pieces. The methods I had chosen to fix my heart only placed patches over the wounds. These patches became hard and crusted so that whenever good tried to penetrate it was pushed away. I wanted to feel love, but I didn't know how. Every remembrance of every situation the enemy had used to destroy me began to surface. I did not know how to deal with the pain.

All I knew was that, according to my view of life, I had been cheated and wronged. Forgiveness was not in my vocabulary. To forgive others and myself I had to deal with each one of my problems. These problems may have been nothing to other people, but pain is pain. It depends on your tolerance level. I was bleeding, but it wasn't a flesh wound. For the bleeding to stop I had to learn the power of forgiveness—that was hard—and how to love myself.

Forgiveness was not an easy area for me to handle. After all, we don't think about it much. We assume that if we don't think about those areas of our lives that have caused undue pain they will go away. I did not know my past had so adversely affected my life. I pretended to be okay. It became easy to act as if my world was fine. Now that I look back, however, I am reminded of the warning signs that something was dreadfully wrong. Those warning signs were reflected in my attitude about myself. I became bitter and a people-pleaser. Lack of self-esteem and self-worth had become my friend. I did what I could to survive, but my life was not really about me. I allowed others to make my choices. I settled and did not strive for what I wanted. I existed, and that was about it. I followed the crowd's lead. I did not see a way out of this lifestyle and thought it must have been my punishment.

My family knew me as the one who always cried growing up. Whenever I didn't get my way I cried. I threw a temper tantrum at the drop of a hat (warning). My tears got me what I wanted. But why was I really crying? It wasn't until later I discovered I cried because I was hurting, but I didn't want anyone to know why.

What exactly was causing the hurt? I would see a couple who appeared to have the ideal relationship and say, "Wow, they must be special people to God." Or I would see a woman pursuing her career and feel that she had what it took to succeed, never realizing I was made out of the same substance she was.

I had not yet learned to activate my source of power. This would begin with forgiveness. All I had to do was pray to God and ask forgiveness for all the wrong I had ever done (guilt) and forgive all who had ever wronged me. "Lord, I forgive" is simple to say but hard to do. One of the greatest lessons I have learned is that cleansing comes from forgiveness. That's right. First John 1:9 states, "If we confess our sins He is faithful and just to forgive us our sins and to cleanse us from all unrighteousness." What we sow in tears, we shall reap in joy. I needed to be cleansed, and I am not talking about a sponge bath. I had a lot of dirt in me that needed to come out.

Chapter 2

Breaking the Fallow Ground

"Sow to yourselves in righteousness, reap in mercy; break up your fallow ground: for it is time to seek the Lord, till he come and rain righteousness upon you."
Hosea 10:12

Fallow ground is that which has been plowed but not sown; it is ground not in use—idle ground crusted over and hardened until it needs to be broken up again to receive the seed. We must break up the ground of our hearts and yield them to God. If I wanted righteousness to rain upon me I had to break up the fallow ground. So again I wept.

I discovered that a lot of my weeping did not come from how I felt people had wronged me, but from how I felt about myself. I had picked up evil habits along the way which were mere weeds growing around my heart. This kept me in a whirlwind of uncertainty, pain and mental anguish.

I had been sowing seeds of discord where there should have been seeds of righteousness. The feeling of not being good enough had taken over. I discovered I was using the wrong fertilizer. Instead of sowing spiritual words of endless possibilities I was sowing words of extreme negativity.

One of the most damaging things you can do to yourself is not to accept who you are. God knew what He was doing when He created you. Accepting who you are is learning to see what God sees. You have been fearfully and wonderfully made by Almighty God, and you can do nothing to change that. You don't have to live up to anyone else's standards.

Breaking the fallow ground meant taking a long look in the mirror. Not a glance, but a long look. I began to look at the imperfections not in my face but in my soul and in my spirit. When I looked into my soul—the seat of my emotions—I found that I was one hot mess. Whew! I was all over the map. I was singing Frank Sinatra's song, "I Did It My Way." My emotions were off the Richter scale. I wanted to be loved, but I didn't love myself. I thought happiness came from another person, and I was not trying to hear what God wanted for my life. I looked good on the outside, but my inside was messed up, as they say. I had to go through the process of learning to love me. I didn't think I was good enough. No one said it to me, but it was what I thought. I had to learn that each of us has to live the life God created for us and not compare it to someone else's life.

Facing the fact that I didn't love myself was hard. The enemy has a way of making you feel bad about yourself by focusing on your imperfections. When I looked at myself, I saw rejection, doubt and fear. I discovered I didn't know how to love me. Loving yourself is developing an attitude of self-respect, protecting your heart and personally caring for your needs. This is the only dependable way to create love in your own life that you can share with others.

I had to learn to discover ways of letting go of the past so I could walk in the present. Learning to define myself by what I had accomplished rather than what I hadn't served as a catapult to get me where I needed to be.

Leviticus 19:18 tells us to love our neighbors as ourselves. This is one of the many places in the Bible that instructs us to love ourselves. This is also found in Galatians 5:14 – "For all the law is fulfilled in one word, *even* in this; Thou shalt love thy neighbour as thyself." We talk about the importance of loving our neighbor, but rarely talk about loving ourselves in the same manner we love them. I cannot in all fairness love my neighbor if I don't love myself. If I love me I should want to take care of me. But isn't it amazing how we can pay more attention to caring for a little plant than for our own personal needs. I have even found it easier to take care of other people's problems and help them find a solution than to take care of my own personal needs.

When I began to break up the fallow pieces of my heart I noticed how peaceful my life was becoming. It was no longer about other people and what they thought. It was about me and the Lord. God showed me everything that had happened in my life was for a purpose. The bitter and the sweet, the good and the bad, were all working together. My afflictions had a purpose.

Chapter 3

Afflictions

"For our light affliction, which is but for a moment, worketh for us a far more exceeding and eternal weight of glory." 2 Corinthians 4:17

We have heard the expression "If it's not one thing, it's another." I have experienced this expression so much that at one point I did not feel the "things" would ever stop. It was one thing after another, and each time I tried to figure out where the affliction was coming from and how I could overcome it. When life sends pain our way, our actions do not always rationalize our thinking. I have often marveled at those who have been in continuous valleys of despair; yet their pursuits of happiness never faded. Unfortunately I was not one of them. My question was, how could a loving God allow us to go through suffering? Could any good come from my afflictions? Psalm 119:17 says, "It was good for me that I had been afflicted so that I might learn your decrees."

Afflictions, according to Webster's dictionary, are "persecutions or the repeated inflicting of suffering or annoyance." My attitude during my affliction determines if I will be the victim or the victor. A view in retrospect has shown me that life does not just happen. If you want something you have to do something. If you want something to change you have to change something, and most of the time the change will be you.

Promiscuity and prowess had left me unable to make decisions for myself. I looked good on the outside, but the inside needed attention. There is now and will continue to be a purpose in our afflictions. That purpose is to teach us and test us. We learn valuable lessons as a result of afflictions. , "God gets his best soldiers from the valleys of affliction." Charles Spurgeon

"Many are the afflictions of the righteous, but the Lord delivereth him out of them all" (Psalm 34:19)Life is filled with "going throughs" and "coming outs." Just know that when you are going through some test or trial you are not alone. In Exodus we read the story of the affliction of the children of Israel. The more they were afflicted, the more they multiplied and grew. God taught me to stay focused on Him not on my afflictions. God is the deliverer. He is the healer. He is the restorer. It's not about what you are going through but Who is bringing you through it.

I had to learn what was causing my afflictions. Some were brought on by disobedience, lack of discipline and self-control, and fear. Disobedience is sin. Sometimes we just need deliverance from bad habits. If God says to stop doing it, He will give you the strength you need to overcome. I was so stubborn. In the Bible we read that stubbornness is like rebellion and rebellion is witchcraft (see I Samuel 15:23). I knew I needed to change some things, but my flesh kept getting in the way. Why was I so hard pressed not to change? I believe it was my defense mechanism. Things that were comfortable for me kept others from hurting me or getting too close.

Another area of suffering came from lack of discipline and spiritual self-control. I wanted what I wanted without counting the cost. A disciplined life is one that is filled with positive reinforcements that keep you moving in the right direction. "The steps of a good man are ordered by the Lord, and he delighteth in his way" (Psalm 37:23). My life lacked discipline. The decisions I made were not based on what God's Word said but on what I wanted. Everything we do has consequences. I had to learn to "think it through." I was a people-pleaser. Remember: I needed people to like me. This meant doing things I may not have agreed with at the time, but it made me happy temporarily.

"No man or woman has achieved an effective personality who is not self-disciplined.

Such discipline must not be an end in itself; but must be directed to the development of resolute Christian character."—John S. Bonnell

Self-control is the ability to control impulses and reactions. It brings and establishes a life of order and not chaos. I had to slow down. I was living my life at a rapid pace thinking that if I didn't do it now something would happen. The Greek word for self-control is *enkrateia,* and its root meaning is power over oneself or self-mastery. I had to develop mastery over my passions.

It is amazing what self-control can do for you. I started taking control over what I ate, how I felt, what I would allow to happen in my life and who would be involved in my life. Take back the control. Peace will become a constant in your life.

For many, many years fear wasn't a problem for me. I grew up as a cry baby, but I was tough. I would fight at the drop of a hat. If there was something going on with my friends all they had to do was come and get me and the fight was on. I could tell a person off in fifteen seconds and leave them standing there asking, "What did she just say?" I had no fear during my early years. I knew what I wanted in life, and I was on my way to get it. I had plans for success, but of course some of the best-made plans don't come to fruition. My life became interrupted by teen pregnancy, death of my daughter at two months of age, alcohol, drugs, marital problems, divorce, debt, robbery-death of my mother, the recent death of my son at thirty-five years old, more debt and robbery at gunpoint, to mention a few. You probably have a list as well.

I began to break down and become fearful of life. It is amazing how people will tell you, "God has not given you a spirit of fear." Well, I had one, and it was causing me problems. I had now become afraid to live my best life. Why? Because fear has a way of making you think a great big world is out there and you can never be a part of it. Fear is designed to grip you and hold you back. Instead of saying, "I can," you will find yourself saying, "I can't."

To correct this problem I began to say, "Oh, yes, I can." "I can finish everything I started." "I am just as good as the next person." "Fear will no longer hold me back." I discovered where it came from, and I sent it back. God had a plan for my life, and I was on the road to finding out what it was.

Chapter 4

Emotions

This I say then, Walk in the Spirit and ye shall not fulfill the lust of the flesh. For the flesh lusteth against the Spirit, and the Spirit again the flesh: and these are contrary the one to the other: so that ye cannot do the things that ye would. Galatians 5:16-17

I had to take back control of my life. This meant wanting only what God wanted for me. I no longer had to pick and choose based on my emotions. That's right. Many of our problems stem from our emotions. Emotions can be like whirlwinds, ever turning, trying to find a place to land. My emotions dictated my life. Don't live your life based on how you feel. Feelings are unpredictable. We have all made decisions based on how we felt, and some of those decisions were not good ones. Emotions control our thinking, behavior and actions. God gave us emotions as part of our souls, but our whole lives should not appear to revolve around the impulses of emotion.

What is in your heart can be evidenced in your emotions. Your heart reveals when you are afraid, when you are discouraged, when you are sad or in need of comfort, when you are convicted of sin and cleansed from sin through God's forgiveness, and when you are rejoicing.

Our emotions emit joy, happiness, cheerfulness, excitement, elation, stimulation, despondency, sorrow, grief, melancholy, misery, moaning, dejection, confusion, anxiety, zeal, coldness, affection, aspiration, covetousness, compassion, kindness, preference, interest, expectation, pride, fear, remorse and hate. You can probably think of some that are not in this list. It's no wonder we get confused. We are out of control.

The various expressions of emotions can be gathered into three groups: 1) affection, 2) desire and 3) feelings. When we overcome these three we are on our way to a path of spiritual maturity.

An emotional life is filled with roller-coaster rides of highs and lows and never stops. I was an emotional wreck. Too many of us have made choices and decisions based on how we loved, what we desired and how we felt. Feelings change. If my life was going to change I had to get a handle on my emotions.

My freedom came from learning that if I was going to live a Spirit-filled life as a believer, my emotions could no longer fluctuate moment by moment or because of what was going on outside of me.

My emotions kept me crying about this and that. When I felt good I cried; when I didn't feel good I cried. My emotions consisted of negative feelings of who I was instead of realizing all God had created me to be. I needed to take my feelings to the cross and allow the Holy Spirit to teach me that although they were part of me they did not have to control me. God had to destroy the fiery nature of my emotions, with its confusion, and subject it totally to spiritual authority. It is the cross of Jesus Christ that gets rid of the confusion of our emotions. I asked God to take control of my emotions, and when He did I no longer needed a pill to keep me stable.

Chapter 5

Love

> *But the fruit of the Spirit is love, joy, peace, longsuffering, gentleness, goodness, faith, meekness, temperance; against such there is no law.* Galatians 5:22-23

> *I sought the Lord, and he heard me, and delivered me from all my fears.* Proverbs 34:4

Learning the true meaning of love is one of the greatest joys you can experience. The love I speak of is not based on how you feel about me or how I feel about you, but how God feels about us. His love is the greatest love of all.

When I discovered how much God loves me, my perspective on life changed.

God's love is unconditional. Our love, however, is usually conditional and is based on how other people behave toward us. It is predicated upon familiarity and direct interaction.

The reason for my weeping did not come from a lack of love from God. It came from my desire to hear the words "I love you." I needed to hear this because I did not love myself.

When you have been abused mentally, physically or both, you develop insecurities about yourself. When you have been rejected you begin to believe something is wrong with you. You feel that you are not good enough to be loved or good enough for the best life has to offer. When your character has been damaged you look for affirmation. Instead of enjoying who you were meant to be your focus changes, and you develop an inferiority complex and low self-esteem.

Learning to love myself has taught me to accept who I am with all of my flaws. I now know it is okay to say no and I don't have to compare myself with others. No one else can do a better job of being me than I can. I don't have to tolerate nonsense, raise grown folk or hide in someone else's shadow. I am who God made me to be. Even though I have experienced some heavy blows in life, I don't have to become a poster child for "destined for failure." With God, failure is not an option.

We must not be blind-sided by false love. True love does not hurt. I stopped looking for love in the wrong places. I am special to God. He loves me, and He wants me to love me. Learn to plant your own garden and give yourself flowers instead of waiting for someone else to do it.

Today represents the first day of the rest of my life. I did nothing to earn it. God saw fit to bless me with it. Therefore I will cherish it as just that. Thank You, God, for believing in me and giving me another chance. The joy I feel within my spirit right now is unexplainable. God has answered my prayer. Wow! It is time to move on. I am a new creature in Christ. Old things are passed away; behold, all things become new.(II Corinthians 5:17) There is still power to my weeping, but it is now under control. My emotions no longer dictate my actions or my decisions. God has repaired the broken places of my heart, and He still delivers me from my afflictions. His love is and always will be the greatest love of all. I could not have completed this journey without Him. God, thank You for loving me more than I could ever know.

I have now become an advocate for change. I pray this book has been a blessing to you and that you too will discover restoration through your tears.

CPSIA information can be obtained at www.ICGtesting.com
Printed in the USA
BVOW041820210213

313891BV00001B/112/P